Winning SPIRITUAL WARFARE

NEIL T. ANDERSON

HARVEST HOUSE PUBLISHERS
Eugene, Oregon 97402

WINNING SPIRITUAL WARFARE
Taken from **THE BONDAGE BREAKER®**
Copyright © 1990 by Harvest House Publishers
Eugene, Oregon 97402
www.harvesthousepublishers.com

ISBN-13: 978-0-89081-868-8

Printed in the United States of America

10 11 12 / VP / 26 25

Contents

1
Free at Last!

♦

A few years ago I was speaking in a Southern California church on the subject of the New Age movement. My text was 1 Timothy 4:1: "The Spirit explicitly says that in later times some will fall away from the faith, paying attention to deceitful spirits and doctrines of demons." After my message I was surrounded at the front of the sanctuary by people wanting to hear more about freedom from spiritual conflicts caused by demonic influences.

Sitting about halfway back in the sanctuary was a 22-year-old woman who had been weeping uncontrollably since the service ended. Several people had tried to comfort her, but she wouldn't allow anyone to get near her. Finally a church staff member cut through the crowd around me and said, "I'm sorry, folks, but we need Dr. Anderson back here right away."

As I approached the young woman I could hear her sobbing, "He understands! He understands!" We were able to get her out of the sanctuary and into a private office. After she calmed down, I scheduled an appointment with her for the next week.

When Nancy arrived for her appointment, she described her horrible childhood, which included an abusive father and a grandmother who identified herself as a black witch. "When I was three years old I received my guardians—spirit guides," she continued.

"They were my companions, telling me how to live and what to say. I never questioned if having spiritual guides was anything but normal until my mother took me to Sunday school. Then I began to suspect that my inner companions might not be good for me. When I asked my parents about it, my father beat me. I never asked again!"

In order to cope with the increasing torment that her spirit guides brought to her life, Nancy resorted to rigid personal discipline. In her high school years she trusted Christ as her Savior. But instead of leaving her, her "guardians" continued to harass her.

After high school Nancy turned to the epitome of discipline: the Marines. Determined to become the toughest of the lady leathernecks, she won awards for her discipline. But her spiritual torment kept pushing her mind and emotions to the edge. She refused to tell anyone about her mental battle for fear that she would be labeled insane. Finally the pressure overcame her and she snapped. Nancy quietly accepted a medical discharge and retreated to a lonely existence of inner turmoil and pain. This was Nancy's condition when she came to church and heard me talk about deceiving spirits.

"Finally someone understands me!" Nancy concluded tearfully.

"Would you like to get rid of your spirit guides?" I asked.

There was a long pause. "Will they really leave, or will I go home and be thrashed by them again?"

"You will be free," I assured her.

An hour later Nancy *was* free—and was hugging us with an openness she had never known before. "Now I can have people over to my house!" she exclaimed joyfully.

The Reality of the Dark Side

Nancy's experience is not an obscure, erratic blip in the contemporary Christian community. In fact, in more than 25 years of ministry as a pastor, counselor, seminary professor, and conference speaker, I have ministered to more Christians in bondage to the dark side of the spiritual world than you may believe.

My own journey into this realm of ministry did not come by choice. I was an aerospace engineer before God called me into ministry. Even as a Christian layman I was never curious about demon activity or the occult. The lure of esoteric knowledge and occultic power never appealed to me.

Yet I have always been disposed to believe what the Bible says about the spiritual world even when it conflicts with accepted opinion. As a result, over 15 years ago the Lord began to direct me to Christians like Nancy who were in bondage to various forms of satanism and the occult. Also, I began to meet many believers who were controlled by thought patterns, habits, and behaviors which blocked their growth. My desire was to see these people free to live productive lives, but my training hadn't equipped me well in this area. I fumbled my way through a lot of failure in my early attempts to minister to them, but I also experienced some surprising success. I have concluded that Christians are woefully unprepared to deal with the dark world of Satan's kingdom or to minister to those who are in bondage to it.

Are you one of those Christians who lives in the quiet desperation of bondage to fear, anger, depression, habits you can't break, thoughts or inner voices you can't elude, or sinful behavior you can't escape? Not every spiritual problem is the result of direct demonic activity. But you may be in bondage because you have overlooked or denied the reality of demonic powers at work in the world today.

God Wants You Mature and Free

Two concepts determine the victory and fruitfulness of a Christian. The first concept is *maturity*. Paul wrote: "We are to grow up in all aspects into Him, who is the head, even Christ ... to a mature man, to the measure of the stature which belongs to the fulness of Christ" (Ephesians 4:15, 13). God has given us everything we need to grow to maturity in Christ (2 Peter 1:3). But Satan is opposed to our maturity and will do anything he can to keep us from realizing who we are in and what we have in Christ. Since we wrestle against principalities and powers instead of flesh and blood (Ephesians 6:12), we must experience victory over the dark side before we can fully mature.

The second concept of the successful Christian life is *freedom*: "It was for freedom that Christ set us free; therefore keep standing firm and do not be subject again to a yoke of slavery" (Galatians 5:1). This verse not only assures us that God wants us free, but warns us that we can lose our freedom.

Before we received Christ, we were slaves to sin. But because of Christ's work on the cross, sin's power over us has been broken. Satan has no right of ownership or authority over us. He is a defeated foe, but he is committed to keeping us from realizing that. He knows he can block your effectiveness as a Christian if he can deceive you into believing that you are nothing but a product of your past, subject to sin, prone to failure, and controlled by your habits. As long as he can confuse you and blind you with his dark lies, you won't be able to see that the chains which once bound you are broken. I don't believe in instant maturity, but I do believe in instant freedom, and I have seen thousands of people set free by the truth. Once a person is free, you would be amazed at how quickly he or she matures!

2
Jesus Has You Covered

✦

I received the following letter during a week-long conference I was conducting on spiritual conflicts. Frances' struggle vividly captures the nature of the spiritual conflict which entangles many Christians:

Dear Dr. Anderson:

I attended your Sunday sessions, but while waiting to talk to you after the Sunday evening meeting I suddenly felt ill. I was burning up like I had a fever, and I got so weak I thought I was going to faint. So I went home.

I need help. I've had more trouble in my life since I became a Christian than I ever had before. I've overdosed on alcohol and drugs so many times I can't count them. I've cut myself several times with razor blades, sometimes very seriously. I have thoughts and feelings and ideas of suicide weekly, like stabbing myself through the heart. I'm a slave to masturbation; I'm out of control, and I don't know how to stop.

On the outside I appear very normal. I have a good job, and I live with an outstanding family in our community. I even work with junior highers at my church. But I can't really explain my relationship with God anymore. I've been seeing a psychiatrist for two years. Sometimes I think I'm this way because of a messed-up childhood, or maybe I was born this way.

How can I tell if my problems are in my mind, or the result of sin and disobedience against God, or the evidence of demonic influence? I would like to talk to you during the conference. But I don't want to try any more remedies that don't work.

– Frances

The confusion in Frances' mind is a clear tip-off that her problem is the result of demonic influence. I met with her that week, and she was as miserable, frustrated, and defeated as she sounds in her letter. She wanted to serve God with all her heart, and she had as much access to the power and authority to resist Satan as you or I do. But she was getting slammed around like a hockey puck by the powers of darkness because she didn't understand her authority or her protection in Christ.

Once Frances began to realize that she was not powerless or defenseless in the battle, and that she could make choices to change her situation, the chains dropped off and she walked free. Her freedom not only changed her life dramatically, but it also affected many others around her for good.

Getting Involved in God's Protection

Have you experienced the reality of Frances' statement: "I've had more trouble in my life since I became a Christian than I ever had before"? When you become a child of God, you gain an enemy you didn't have before. In your B.C. days (before Christ), the god of this world didn't bother with you because you were already part of his kingdom. His goal was to keep you there by blinding you to God's provision for your salvation (2 Corinthians 4:3,4). But when you came to life in Christ, Satan didn't curl up his tail and pull in his fangs. He is still committed to foul up your life through his deception to "prove" that Christianity doesn't work, that God's Word isn't true, and that nothing really happened when you were born again.

"So what's the benefit of being a Christian? Who in his right mind would want to sign up for a life of trouble?" you may wonder. In reality, it doesn't need to be a life of trouble. You don't have to be a defenseless hockey puck at the mercy of Satan and his demons. God has already supplied the protection you need to ward off any and every attack in the spiritual realm. You just need to know what God has provided and to apply it to your own experience.

Some Christians are a little paranoid about evil powers, suspecting that demons lurk around every corner just waiting to possess them. That's an unfounded fear. Our relationship to demonic powers in the spiritual realm is a lot like our relationship to germs in the physical realm. We know that germs are all around us: in the air, in the water, in our food, in other people, even in us. But do you live in constant fear of catching some disease? No—unless you're a hypochondriac! You know enough about wellness to eat the right foods, get enough rest, and keep yourself and your possessions clean. If you happen to catch a cold or get the measles, you simply deal with the problem and go on with your life.

It's the same in the spiritual realm. Demons are like little invisible germs looking for someone to infect. We are never told in Scripture to be afraid of them. You just need to be aware of their reality and commit yourself to live a righteous life in spite of them. Should you come under attack, deal with it and go on with life. Remember: The only thing big about a demon is its mouth. Demons are habitual liars. In Jesus Christ, the Truth, you are equipped with all the authority and protection you need to deal with anything they throw at you.

The Christian's Magna Charta of protection is Ephesians 6:10-18. The first thing you should see in this passage about receiving God's protection is that our role is not passive. God requires us to be active participants in the spiritual defense that He has provided for us. Notice how often we are commanded to take an active role (emphasis added):

> Finally, be strong in the Lord and in the strength of His might. Put on the full armor of God, that you may be able to stand firm against the schemes of the devil. For our struggle is not against flesh and blood, but against the rulers, against the powers, against the world forces of this darkness, against the spiritual forces of wickedness in the heavenly places. Therefore, take up the full armor of God, that you may be able to resist in the evil day, and having done everything, to stand firm (verses 10-13).

You may be wondering, "If my position in Christ is secure and my protection is found in Him, why do I have to get actively involved? Can't I just rest in Him and let Him protect me?" That's like a soldier saying, "Our country is a major military power. We have the most advanced tanks, planes, missiles, and ships in the world. Why should I bother with wearing a helmet, standing guard, or learning how to shoot a gun? It's much more comfortable to stay in camp while the tanks and planes fight the war." When the enemy troops infiltrate, guess who will be one of the first soldiers to get picked off!

God, our "commanding officer," has provided everything we need to secure victory over the evil forces of darkness. But He says, "I've prepared a winning strategy and designed effective weapons. But if you don't do your part by staying on active duty, you're likely to become a casualty." In her classic book War on the Saints, Jessie Penn-Lewis stated: "The chief condition for the working of evil spirits in a human being, apart from sin, is passivity, in exact opposition to the condition which God requires from His children for His working in them." You can't expect God to protect you from demonic influences if you don't take an active part in His prepared strategy.

Dressed for Success

A primary element in our protection is the armor that God has provided for us and instructed us to put on. Paul wrote:

> Stand firm therefore, having girded your loins with truth, and having put on the breastplate of righteousness, and having shod your feet with the preparation of the gospel of peace; in addition to all, taking up the shield of faith with which you will be able to extinguish all the flaming missiles of the evil one. And take the helmet of salvation, and the sword of the Spirit, which is the word of God (Ephesians 6:14-17).

When we put on the armor of God we are really putting on Christ (Romans 13:12-14). And when we put on Christ we take ourselves out of the realm of the flesh, where we are vulnerable to attack, and we place ourselves within the dominion of Christ, where the evil one cannot touch us. Satan has nothing in Christ (John 14:30), and to the extent that we put on Christ, the evil one cannot touch us (1 John 5:18). He can only touch that which is on his own level. That's why we are commanded, "Make no provision for the flesh" (Romans 13:14), meaning "Don't live on Satan's level."

Though the armor of God is readily available and our eternal destiny is secure, we are still vulnerable to Satan's accusations, temptations, and deceptions. If we give in to these, we can be influenced by Satan's wishes (Galatians 5:1). And if we remain under his influence long enough, we can lose control. Yes, believers can be controlled by Satan if they fail to stand against him. *Ownership* is never at stake, however. We belong to God, and Satan can't touch our basic identity in Him. But as long as we are living in this body, we can allow ourselves to be vulnerable targets for all his fiery darts.

3
The Powers That Be

✦

Virtually all evangelical Christians and even many liberals agree that Satan is a living being who is responsible for the evil in the world today. Many confessions of faith used to include a section about believing in a personal devil – not that every person has his own personal devil, but that the devil is an actual personage rather than merely an impersonal force. But when you start talking about demons being alive and active in the world today, a lot of Christians bristle, "Hold on there. I believe in the devil, but I don't buy that stuff about demons."

My question to these people is: How do you think Satan carries on his worldwide ministry of evil and deception? He is a created being. He is not omnipresent, omniscient, or omnipotent. He can't be everywhere in the world tempting and deceiving millions of people at the same moment. He does so through an army of emissaries (demons, evil spirits, fallen angels, etc.) who propagate his plan of rebellion around the world.

Disbelief in personal demonic activity (or an inordinate fear of demons) is further evidence of the static that Satan perpetrates in our minds to distort the truth. In the classic *Screwtape Letters*, C.S. Lewis wrote: "There are two equal and opposite errors into which our race can fall about the devils. One is to disbelieve their existence. The other is to believe and feel an unhealthy interest in them. They themselves are equally pleased by both errors and hail a materialist or a magician with the same delight.[1]

Running the Gauntlet of Evil

The Bible does not attempt to prove the existence of demons any more than it attempts to prove the existence of God. It simply reports on their activities as if its first readers accepted their existence. Perhaps the best description of the spiritual host which harasses God's people is found in Ephesians 6:12: "Our struggle is not against flesh and blood, but against the rulers, against the powers, against the world forces of this darkness, against the spiritual forces of wickedness in the heavenly places."

How do these evil spirits interfere with our lives? Let me answer with a simple illustration. Imagine that you are standing at one end of a long, narrow street lined on both sides with two-story row houses. At the other end of the street stands Jesus Christ, and your Christian life is the process of walking down that long street of maturity in Him. There is absolutely nothing in the street which can keep you from reaching Jesus. So, when you receive Christ, you fix your eyes on Him and start walking.

But since this world is still under the dominion of Satan, the row houses on either side of you are inhabited by beings who are committed to keeping you from reaching your goal. They have no power or authority to block your path or even slow your step, so they hang out of the windows and call to you, hoping to turn your attention away from your goal and disrupt your progress.

One of the ways they will try to distract you is by calling out, "Hey, look over here! I've got something you really want. It tastes good, feels good, and is a lot

---

1. C.S. Lewis, *The Screwtape Letters* (Old Tappan, NJ: Fleming H. Revell, 1978).

more fun than your boring walk down the street. Come on in and take a look." That's temptation, suggesting to your mind ways to serve yourself instead of God.

As you continue your walk toward Christ you will also have thoughts like "I'm stupid. I'm ugly. I'll never amount to anything for God." Satan's emissaries are masters at accusation, especially after they have distracted you through temptation. One minute they're saying, "Try this; there's nothing wrong with it." Then, when you yield, they're right there taunting, "See what you did! How can you call yourself a Christian when you behave like that?" Accusation is one of Satan's primary weapons in his attempt to distract you from your goal.

Other remarks which are hurled at you as you walk down the street sound like this: "You don't need to go to church today. It's not important to pray and read the Bible every day. Some of the New Age stuff isn't so bad." That's deception, and it is Satan's most subtle and debilitating weapon. You will often hear these messages in first-person singular: "I don't need to go to church today, pray, read my Bible," etc. Satan knows you will be more easily deceived if he can make you think the thought was yours instead of his.

What is the enemy's goal in having his demons jeer you, taunt you, lure you, and question you from the windows and doorways along your path? He wants you to slow down, stop, sit down, and if possible, give up your journey toward Christ. He wants to influence you to doubt your ability to believe and serve God. Remember: He has absolutely no power or authority to keep you from steadily progressing in your walk toward Christ. And he can never again own you, because you have been redeemed by Jesus Christ and you are forever in Him (1 Peter 1:18, 19). But if he can get you to listen to the thoughts he plants in your mind, he can influence you. And if you allow him to influence you long enough through temptation, accusation, and deception, he can control you.

4
Steps to Freedom in Christ

◆

Prayer

Dear Heavenly Father,

We acknowledge Your presence in this room and in our lives. You are the only omniscient (all knowing), omnipotent (all powerful), and omnipresent (always present) God. We are dependent upon You for apart from You we can do nothing. We stand in the truth that all authority in heaven and on earth has been given to the resurrected Christ, and because we are in Christ, we share that authority in order to make disciples and set captives free. We ask You to fill us with Your Holy Spirit and lead us into all truth. We pray for Your complete protection and ask for Your guidance. In Jesus' name. Amen.

Declaration

In the name and authority of the Lord Jesus Christ, we command Satan and all evil spirits to release (<u>name</u>) in order that (<u>name</u>) can be free to know and choose to do the will of God. As children of God seated with Christ in the heavenlies, we agree that every enemy of the Lord Jesus Christ be bound to silence. We say to Satan and all his evil workers that "you cannot inflict any pain or in any way prevent God's will from being accomplished in (<u>name's</u>) life."

Preparation

Before going through the *Steps to Freedom*, review the events of your life to discern specific areas that might need to be addressed.

Family History

_____ Religious history of parents and grandparents
_____ Home life from childhood through high school
_____ History of physical or emotional illness in the family
_____ Adoption, foster care, guardians

Personal History

_____ Eating habits (bulimia, bingeing and purging, anorexia, compulsive eating)
_____ Addictions (drugs, alcohol)
_____ Prescription medications (what for?)
_____ Sleeping patterns and nightmares
_____ Raped or any sexual, physical, emotional abuse
_____ Thought life (obsessive, blasphemous, condemning, distracting thoughts, poor concentration, fantasy)
_____ Mental interference in church, prayer, or Bible study
_____ Emotional life (anger, anxiety, depression, bitterness, fears)
_____ Spiritual journey (salvation: when, how, and assurance)

Now you are ready to begin. The following are seven specific steps to process in order to experience freedom from your past. You will address the areas where Satan most commonly takes advantage of us and where strongholds have been built. Christ purchased your victory when He shed His blood for you on the cross. Realizing your freedom will be the result of what you choose to believe, confess, forgive, renounce, and forsake. No one can do that for you. The battle for your mind can only be won as you personally choose truth.

As you go through these *Steps to Freedom*, remember that Satan will only be defeated if you confront him verbally. He cannot read your mind and is under no obligation to obey your thoughts. Only God has complete knowledge of your mind. As you process each step, it is important that you submit to God inwardly and resist the devil by reading aloud each prayer—verbally renouncing, forgiving, confessing, etc.

You are taking a fierce moral inventory and making a rock-solid commitment to truth. If your problems stem from a source other than those covered in these steps, you have nothing to lose by going through them. If you are sincere, the only thing that can happen is that you will get very right with God!

STEP 1:
Counterfeit vs. Real

The first step to freedom in Christ is to renounce your previous or current involvement with satanically-inspired occult practices and false religions. You need to renounce any activity and group which denies Jesus Christ, offers guidance through any source other than the absolute authority of the written Word of God, or requires secret initiations, ceremonies, or covenants.

In order to help you assess your spiritual experiences, begin this step by asking God to reveal false guidance and counterfeit religious experiences.

Dear Heavenly Father,
I ask You to guard my heart and my mind and reveal to me any and all involvement I have had either knowingly or unknowingly with cultic or occult practices, false religions, and false teachers. In Jesus' name, I pray. Amen.

Using the "Non-Christian Spiritual Experience Inventory" on the following page, carefully check anything in which you were involved. This list is not exhaustive, but it will guide you in identifying non-Christian experiences. Add any additional involvement you have had. Even if you "innocently" participated in something or observed it, you should write it on your list to renounce, just in case you unknowingly gave Satan a foothold.

Non-Christian Spiritual Experience Inventory

(Please check those that apply.)

__ Astral-projection
__ Ouija board
__ Table or body lifting
__ Dungeons and Dragons
__ Speaking in trance
__ Automatic writing
__ Magic eight ball
__ Telepathy
__ Using spells or curses
__ Seance
__ Materialization
__ Clairvoyance
__ Spirit guides
__ Fortune telling
__ Tarot cards
__ Palm reading
__ Astrology/horoscopes
__ Rod & pendulum (dowsing)
__ Self-hypnosis
__ Mental manipulations or attempts to swap minds
__ Black and white magic
__ New Age medicine
__ Blood pacts or cut yourself in a destructive way
__ Fetishism (objects of worship, crystals, good luck charms)
__ Incubi and succubi (sexual spirits)
__ Other _____
__ Christian Science
__ Unity
__ The Way International

__ Unification Church
__ Mormonism
__ Church of the Living Word
__ Jehovah's Witnesses
__ Children of God (Love)
__ Swedenborgianism
__ Unitarianism
__ Masons
__ New Age
__ The Forum (EST)
__ Spirit worship
__ Other _____
__ Buddhism
__ Hare Krishna
__ Bahaism
__ Rosicrucian
__ Science of the Mind
__ Science of Creative Intelligence
__ Transcendental Meditation
__ Hinduism
__ Yoga
__ Echkankar
__ Roy Masters
__ Silva Mind Control
__ Father Divine
__ Theosophical Society
__ Islam
__ Black Muslim
__ Religion of Martial Arts
__ Other _____

• Have you ever been hypnotized, attended a New Age or parapsychology seminar, consulted a medium, Spiritist, or channeler? Explain.

• Do you or have you ever had an imaginary friend or spirit guide offering you guidance or companionship? Explain.

• Have you ever heard voices in your mind or had repeating and nagging thoughts condemning you or that were foreign to what you believe or feel, like there was a dialog going on in your head? Explain.

• What other spiritual experiences have you had that would be considered out of the ordinary?

• Have you ever made a vow, covenant, or pact with any individual or group other than God?

• Have you been involved in satanic ritual or satanic worship in any form? Explain.

When you are confident that your list is complete, confess and renounce each involvement whether active or passive by praying aloud the following prayer, repeating it separately for each item on your list:

> Lord,
> I confess that I have participated in_____ and I renounce_____. Thank you that in Christ I am forgiven.

If there has been any involvement in satanic ritual or heavy occult activity, you need to state aloud the following special renunciations which apply. Read across the page, renouncing the first item in the column on the Kingdom of Darkness and then affirming the first truth in the column on the Kingdom of Light. Continue down the page in this manner.

All satanic rituals, covenants, and assignments must be specifically renounced as the Lord allows you to recall them. Some who have been subjected to satanic ritual abuse may have developed multiple personalities in order to survive. Nevertheless, continue through the *Steps to Freedom* in order to resolve all that you consciously can. It is important that you resolve the demonic strongholds first. Every personality must resolve his/her issues and agree to come together in Christ. You may need someone who understands spiritual conflict to help you maintain control and not be deceived into false memories. Only Jesus can bind up the broken-hearted, set captives free, and make us whole.

Special Renunciations for Satanic Ritual Involvement

Kingdom of Darkness

— I renounce ever signing my name over to Satan or having had my name signed over to Satan.
— I renounce any ceremony where I may have been wed to Satan.
— I renounce any and all covenants that I made with Satan.
— I renounce all satanic assignments for my life, including duties, marriage, and children.
— I renounce all spirit guides assigned to me.
— I renounce ever giving of my blood in the service of Satan.
— I renounce ever eating of flesh or drinking of blood for satanic worship.
— I renounce any and all guardians and Satanist parents who were assigned to me.
— I renounce any baptism in blood or urine whereby I am identified with Satan.
— I renounce any and all sacrifices that were made on my behalf by which Satan may claim ownership of me.

Kingdom of Light

- I announce that my name is now written in the Lamb's Book of Life.
- I announce that I am the bride of Christ.
- I announce that I am a partaker of the New Covenant with Christ.
- I announce and commit myself to know and do only the will of God and accept only His guidance.
- I announce and accept only the leading of the Holy Spirit.
- I trust only in the shed blood of my Lord Jesus Christ.
- By faith I eat only the flesh and drink only the blood of Jesus in Holy Communion.
- I announce that God is my Father and the Holy Spirit is my Guardian by which I am sealed.
- I announce that I have been baptized into Christ Jesus and my identity is now in Christ.
- I announce that only the sacrifice of Christ has any hold on me.
- I belong to Him. I have been purchased by the blood of the Lamb.

STEP 2:
Deception vs. Truth

Truth is the revelation of God's Word, but we need to acknowledge the truth in the inner self (Ps. 51:6). When David lived a lie, he suffered greatly. When he finally found freedom by acknowledging the truth, he wrote: "How blessed is the man . . . in whose spirit there is no deceit" (Ps. 32:2). We are to lay aside falsehood and speak the truth in love (Eph. 4:15, 25). A mentally healthy person is one who is in touch with reality and relatively free of anxiety. Both qualities should characterize the Christian who renounces deception and embraces the truth.

Begin this critical step by expressing aloud the following prayer. Don't let the enemy accuse you with thoughts such as: "This isn't going to work" or "I wish I could believe this but I can't" or any other lies in opposition to what you are proclaiming. Even if you have difficulty doing so, you need to pray the prayer and read the Doctrinal Affirmation.

> Dear Heavenly Father,
>
> I know that You desire truth in the inner self and that facing this truth is the way of liberation (John 8:32). I acknowledge that I have been deceived by the father of lies (John 8:44) and that I have deceived myself (1 John 1:8). I pray in the name of the Lord Jesus Christ that You, Heavenly Father, will rebuke all deceiving spirits by virtue of the shed blood and resurrection of the Lord Jesus Christ. By faith I have received You into my life and I am now seated with Christ in the heavenlies (Eph. 2:6). I acknowledge that I have the responsibility and authority to resist the devil, and when I do, he will flee from me. I now ask the Holy Spirit to guide me into all truth (John 16:13). I ask You to "Search me, O God, and know my heart; try me and know my anxious thoughts; and see if there be any hurtful way in me, and lead me in the everlasting way" (Ps. 139:23-24). In Jesus' name, I pray. Amen.

You may want to pause at this point to consider some of Satan's deceptive schemes. In addition to false teachers, false prophets, and deceiving spirits, you can deceive yourself. Now that you are alive in Christ and forgiven, you never have to live a lie or defend yourself. Christ is your defense. How have you deceived or attempted to defend yourself according to the following?

Self-deception

__ Hearing God's Word but not doing it (Jas. 1:22; 4:17)
__ Saying we have no sin (1 John 1:8)
__ Thinking we are something when we aren't (Gal. 6:3)
__ Thinking we are wise in our own eyes (1 Cor. 3:18-19)
__ Thinking we will not reap what we sow (Gal. 6:7)

__ Thinking the unrighteous will inherit the Kingdom (1 Cor. 6:9)
__ Thinking we can associate with bad company and not be corrupted (1 Cor. 15:33)

Self-defense
(defending ourselves instead of trusting in Christ)

__ Denial (conscious or subconscious refusal to face the truth)
__ Fantasy (escape from the real world)
__ Emotional insulation (withdraw to avoid rejection)
__ Regression (reverting back to a less threatening time)
__ Displacement (taking out frustrations on others)
__ Projection (blaming others)
__ Rationalization (making excuses for poor behavior)

For those things that have been true in your life, pray aloud:

> Lord,
> I agree that I have been deceived in the area of
> _____. Thank You for forgiving me. I commit
> myself to know and follow Your truth. Amen.

Choosing the truth may be difficult if you have been living a lie (been deceived) for many years. You may need to seek professional help to weed out the defense mechanisms you have depended upon to survive. The Christian needs only one defense—Jesus. Knowing that you are forgiven and accepted as God's child is what sets you free to face reality and declare your dependence on Him.

Faith is the biblical response to the truth, and believing the truth is a choice. When someone says, "I want to believe God, but I just can't," they are being deceived. Of course you can believe God. Faith is something you decide to do, not something you feel like doing. Believing the truth doesn't make it true. It's true; therefore, we believe it. The New Age movement is distorting the truth by saying we create reality through what we believe. We can't create reality with our minds; we face reality. It's what or who you believe in that counts. Everybody believes in something, and everybody walks by faith according to what he or she believes. But if what you believe isn't true, then how you live (walk by faith) won't be right.

Historically, the church has found great value in publicly declaring its beliefs. The Apostles' Creed and the Nicene Creed have been recited for centuries. Read aloud the following affirmation of faith, and do so again as often as necessary to renew your mind. Experiencing difficulty in reading this affirmation may indicate where you are being deceived and under attack. Boldly affirm your commitment to biblical truth.

Doctrinal Affirmation

I recognize that there is only one true and living God (Ex. 20:2-3) who exists as the Father, Son, and Holy Spirit and that He is worthy of all honor, praise, and glory as the Creator, Sustainer, and Beginning and End of all things (Rev. 4:11; 5:9-10; Is. 43:1, 7, 21).

I recognize Jesus Christ as the Messiah, the Word who became flesh and dwelt among us (John 1:1, 14). I believe that He came to destroy the works of Satan (1 John 3:8), that He disarmed the rulers and authorities and made a public display of them, having triumphed over them (Col. 2:15).

I believe that God has proven His love for me because when I was still a sinner, Christ died for me (Rom. 5:8). I believe that He delivered me from the domain of darkness and transferred me to His kingdom, and in Him I have redemption, the forgiveness of sins (Col. 1:13-14).

I believe that I am now a child of God (1 John 3:1-3) and that I am seated with Christ in the heavenlies (Eph. 2:6). I believe that I was saved by the grace of God through faith, that it was a gift, and not the result of any works on my part (Eph. 2:8-9).

I choose to be strong in the Lord and in the strength of His might (Eph. 6:10). I put no confidence in the flesh (Phil. 3:3) for the weapons of warfare are not of the flesh (2 Cor. 10:4). I put on the whole armor of God (Eph. 6:10-20), and I resolve to stand firm in my faith and resist the evil one.

I believe that apart from Christ I can do nothing (John 15:5), so I declare myself dependent on Him. I choose to abide in Christ in order to bear much fruit and glorify the Lord (John 15:8). I announce to Satan that Jesus is my Lord (1 Cor. 12:3), and I reject any counterfeit gifts or works of Satan in my life.

I believe that the truth will set me free (John 8:32) and that walking in the light is the only path of fellowship (1 John 1:7). Therefore, I stand against Satan's deception by taking every thought captive in obedience to Christ (2 Cor. 10:5). I declare that the Bible is the only authoritative standard (2 Tim. 3:15-16). I choose to speak the truth in love (Eph. 4:15).

I choose to present my body as an instrument of righteousness, a living and holy sacrifice, and I renew my mind by the living Word of God in order that I may prove that the will of God is good, acceptable, and perfect (Rom. 6:13; 12:1-2). I put off the old self with its evil practices and put on the new self (Col. 3:9-10), and I declare myself to be a new creature in Christ (2 Cor. 5:17).

I trust my heavenly Father to fill me with His Holy Spirit (Eph. 5:18), to lead me into all truth (John 16:13), and to empower my life that I may live above sin and not carry out the desires of the flesh (Gal. 5:16). I crucify the flesh (Gal. 5:24) and choose to walk by the Spirit.

I renounce all selfish goals and choose the ultimate goal of love (1 Tim. 1:5). I choose to obey the two greatest commandments, to love the Lord my God with all my heart, soul, and mind, and to love my neighbor as myself (Matt. 22:37-39).

I believe that Jesus has all authority in heaven and on earth (Matt. 28:18) and that He is the head over all rule and authority (Col. 2:10). I believe that Satan and his demons are subject to me in Christ since I am a member of Christ's body (Eph. 1:19-23). Therefore, I obey the command to submit to God and to resist the devil (Jas. 4:7), and I command Satan in the name of Christ to leave my presence.

STEP 3:
Bitterness vs. Forgiveness

We need to forgive others in order to be free from our past and not allow Satan to take advantage of us (2 Cor. 2:10-11). We are to be merciful just as our heavenly Father is merciful (Luke 6:36). We are to forgive as we have been forgiven (Eph. 4:31-32). Ask God to bring to mind the names of those people you need to forgive by expressing the following prayer aloud:

> Dear Heavenly Father,
> I thank You for the riches of Your kindness, forbearance, and patience, knowing that Your kindness has led me to repentance (Rom. 2:4). I confess that I have not extended that same patience and kindness toward others who have offended me, but instead I have harbored bitterness and resentment. I pray that during this time of self-examination You would bring to my mind those people I need to forgive in order that I may do so (Matt. 18:35). I ask this in the precious name of Jesus. Amen.

As names come to mind, make a list of only the names. At the end of your list, write "myself." Forgiving yourself is accepting God's cleansing and forgiveness. Also, write "thoughts against God." Thoughts raised up against the knowledge of God will usually result in angry feelings toward Him. Technically, we don't forgive God because He cannot commit any sin of commission or omission. But we need to specifically renounce false expectations and thoughts about God and agree to release any anger we have toward Him.

Before you pray to forgive these people, stop and consider what forgiveness is, what it is not, what decision you will be making, and what the consequences will be. In the following explanation, the main points are in bold print:

Forgiveness is not forgetting. People who try to forget find they cannot. God says He will remember our sins "no more" (Heb. 10:17), but God, being omniscient, cannot forget. Remember our sins "no more" means that God will never use the past against us (Ps. 103:12). Forgetting may be the result of forgiveness, but it is never the means of forgiveness. When we bring up the past against others, we are saying we haven't forgiven them.

Forgiveness is a choice, a crisis of the will. Since God requires us to forgive, it is something we can do. But forgiveness is difficult for us because it pulls against our concept of justice. We want revenge for offenses suffered. However, we are told never to take our own revenge (Rom. 12:19). You say, "Why should I let them off the hook?" That is precisely the problem. You are still hooked to them, still bound by your past. *You will let them off your hook, but they are never off God's.* He will deal with them fairly, something we cannot do.

You say, "You don't understand how much this person hurt me!" But don't you see, they are still hurting you! How do you stop the pain? *You don't forgive someone for their sake; you do it for your own sake so you can be free. Your need to forgive isn't an issue between you and the offender; it's between you and God.*

Forgiveness is agreeing to live with the consequences of another person's sin. Forgiveness is costly. You pay the price of the evil you forgive.

You're going to live with those consequences whether you want to or not; your only choice is whether you will do so in the bitterness of unforgiveness or the freedom of forgiveness. Jesus took the consequences of your sin upon Himself. All true forgiveness is substitutionary, because no one really forgives without bearing the consequences of the other person's sin. God the Father "made Him who knew no sin to be sin on our behalf, that we might become the righteousness of God in Him" (2 Cor. 5:21). Where is the justice? It's the cross that makes forgiveness legally and morally right: "For the death that He died, He died to sin, once for all" (Rom. 6:10).

Decide that you will bear the burdens of their offenses by not using that information against them in the future. This doesn't mean that you tolerate sin. You must set up scriptural boundaries to prevent future abuse. Some may be required to testify for the sake of justice but not for the purpose of seeking revenge from a bitter heart.

How do you forgive from your heart? You acknowledge the hurt and the hate. If your forgiveness doesn't visit the emotional core of your life, it will be incomplete. Many feel the pain of interpersonal offenses, but they won't or don't know how to acknowledge it. Let God bring the pain to the surface so He can deal with it. This is where the healing takes place.

Don't wait to forgive until you feel like forgiving; you will never get there. Feelings take time to heal after the choice to forgive is made and Satan has lost his place (Eph. 4:26-27). *Freedom is what will be gained, not a feeling.*

As you pray, God may bring to mind offending people and experiences you have totally forgotten. Let Him do it even if it is painful. Remember, you are doing this for your sake. God wants you to be free. Don't rationalize or explain the offender's behavior.

Forgiveness is dealing with your pain and leaving the other person to God. Positive feelings will follow in time; freeing yourself from the past is the critical issue right now.

Don't say, "Lord, please help me to forgive," because He is already helping you. Don't say, "Lord, I want to forgive," because you are bypassing the hard-core choice to forgive which is your responsibility. Stay with each individual until you are sure you have dealt with all the remembered pain—what they did, how they hurt you, how they made you feel (rejected, unloved, unworthy, dirty, etc.)

You are now ready to forgive the people on your list so you can be free in Christ with those people no longer having any control over you. For each person on your list, pray aloud:

> Lord,
> I forgive (name the person) for (verbally share every hurt and pain the Lord brings to your mind and how it made you feel).

After you have forgiven every person for every painful memory, then finish this step by praying:

> Lord,
> I release all these people to You and my right to seek revenge. I choose not to hold on to my bitterness and anger, and I ask You to heal my damaged emotions. In Jesus' name, I pray. Amen.

STEP 4:
Rebellion vs. Submission

We live in rebellious times. Many believe it is their right to sit in judgment of those in authority over them. Rebelling against God and His authority gives Satan an opportunity to attack. As our commanding general, the Lord says, "Get into ranks and follow

Me. I will not lead you into temptation, but I will deliver you from evil" (Matt. 6:13).

We have two biblical responsibilities in regard to authority figures: Pray for them and submit to them. The only time God permits us to disobey earthly leaders is when they require us to do something morally wrong before God or attempt to rule outside the realm of their authority. Pray the following prayer:

> Dear Heavenly Father,
>
> You have said that rebellion is as the sin of witchcraft and insubordination is as iniquity and idolatry (1 Sam. 15:23). I know that in action and attitude I have sinned against You with a rebellious heart. I ask Your forgiveness for my rebellion and pray that by the shed blood of the Lord Jesus Christ all ground gained by evil spirits because of my rebelliousness will be canceled. I pray that You will shed light on all my ways that I may know the full extent of my rebelliousness. I now choose to adopt a submissive spirit and a servant's heart. In the name of Christ Jesus, my Lord. Amen.

Being under authority is an act of faith. You are trusting God to work through His established lines of authority. There are times when employers, parents, and husbands are violating the laws of civil government which are ordained by God to protect innocent people against abuse. In these cases, you need to appeal to the state for your protection. In many states, the law requires such abuse to be reported.

In difficult cases, such as continuing abuse at home, further counseling help may be needed. And, in some cases, when earthly authorities have abused their position and are requiring disobedience to God or a compromise in your commitment to Him, you need to obey God, not man.

We are all admonished to submit to one another as equals in Christ (Eph. 5:21). However, there are specific lines of authority in Scripture for the purpose of accomplishing common goals.

Civil Government (Rom. 13:1-7; 1 Tim. 2:1-4; 1 Pet. 2:13-17)
Parents (Eph. 6:1-3)
Husband (1 Pet. 3:1-4) or Wife (Eph. 5:21; 1 Pet. 3:7)
Employer (1 Pet. 2:18-23)
Church Leaders (Heb. 13:17)
God (Dan. 9:5, 9)

Examine each area and ask God to forgive you for those times you have not been submissive, and pray:

Lord,
I agree I have been rebellious toward _____.
I choose to be submissive and obedient to your Word.
In Jesus' name. Amen.

Step 5: Pride vs. Humility

Pride is a killer. Pride says, "I can do it! I can get myself out of this mess without God or anyone else's help." Oh no we can't! We absolutely need God, and we desperately need each other. Paul wrote: "We worship in the Spirit of God and glory in Christ Jesus and put no confidence in the flesh" (Phil. 3:3). Humility is confidence properly placed. We are to be "strong in the Lord and in the strength of His might" (Eph. 6:10). James 4:6-10 and 1 Peter 5:1-10 reveal that spiritual conflict follows pride. Use the following prayer to express your commitment to live humbly before God:

Dear Heavenly Father,
You have said that pride goes before destruction and an arrogant spirit before stumbling (Prov. 16:18). I confess that I have lived independently and have not denied myself, picked up my cross daily, and followed You (Matt. 16:24). In so doing, I have given ground to the enemy in my life. I have believed that I could be

successful and live victoriously by my own strength and resources. I now confess that I have sinned against You by placing my will before Yours and by centering my life around self instead of You. I now renounce the self-life and by so doing cancel all the ground that has been gained in my members by the enemies of the Lord Jesus Christ. I pray that You will guide me so that I will do nothing from selfishness or empty conceit, but with humility of mind I will regard others as more important than myself (Phil. 2:3). Enable me through love to serve others and in honor prefer others (Rom. 12:10). I ask this in the name of Christ Jesus, my Lord. Amen.

Having made that commitment, now allow God to show you any specific areas of your life where you have been prideful, such as:

— having a stronger desire to do my will than God's will;
— being more dependent upon my strengths and re-sources than God's;
— too often believing that my ideas and opinions are better than others;
— being more concerned about controlling others than developing self-control;
— sometimes considering myself more important than others;
— having a tendency to think I have no needs;
— finding it difficult to admit I was wrong;
— having a tendency to be more of a people-pleaser than a God-pleaser;
— being overly concerned about getting the credit I deserve;
— being driven to obtain the recognition that comes from degrees, titles, positions;
— often thinking I am more humble than others;
— these other ways: _____

For each of these that has been true in your life, pray aloud:

Lord,

I agree I have been prideful by _____. I choose to humble myself and place all my confidence in You. Amen.

Step 6:
Bondage vs. Freedom

The next step to freedom deals with habitual sin. People who have been caught in the trap of sin-confess-sin-confess may need to follow the instructions of James 5:16, "Confess your sins to one another, and pray for one another, so that you may be healed. The effective prayer of a righteous man can accomplish much." Seek out a righteous person who will hold you up in prayer and to whom you can be accountable. Others may only need the assurance of 1 John 1:9: "If we confess our sins, He is faithful and righteous to forgive us our sins and to cleanse us from all unrighteousness." Confession is not saying "I'm sorry"; it's saying "I did it." Whether you need the help of others or just the accountability of God, pray the following prayer:

> Dear Heavenly Father,
>
> You have told us to put on the Lord Jesus Christ and make no provision for the flesh in regard to its lust (Rom. 13:14). I acknowledge that I have given in to fleshly lusts which wage war against my soul (1 Pet. 2:11). I thank You that in Christ my sins are forgiven, but I have transgressed Your holy law and given the enemy an opportunity to wage war in my physical body (Rom. 6:12-13; Eph 4:27; Jas. 4:1; 1 Pet. 5:8). I come before Your presence to acknowledge these sins and to seek Your cleansing (1 John 1:9) that I may be freed from the bondage of sin. I now ask You to reveal to my mind the ways that I have transgressed Your moral law and grieved the Holy Spirit. In Jesus' precious name, I pray. Amen.

The deeds of the flesh are numerous. Many of the following issues are from Galatians 5:19-21. Check those that apply to you and any others you have struggled with that the Lord has brought to your mind. Then confess each one with the concluding prayer. Note: sexual sins, eating disorders, substance abuse, abortion, suicidal tendencies, and perfectionism will be dealt with later.

__ stealing	__ cheating
__ lying	__ gossiping
__ fighting	__ controlling
__ jealousy	__ procrastinating
__ envying	__ swearing
__ outbursts of anger	__ greedy
__ complaining	__ lazy
__ criticizing	__ divisive
__ lusting	__ other_____

Dear Heavenly Father,
   I thank You that my sins are forgiven in Christ, but I have walked by the flesh and therefore sinned by _____. Thank You for cleansing me of all unrighteousness. I ask that You would enable me to walk by the Spirit and not carry out the desires of the flesh. In Jesus' name, I pray. Amen.

It is our responsibility not to allow sin to reign in our mortal bodies by not using our bodies as an instrument of unrighteousness (Rom. 6:12-13). If you are or have struggled with sexual sins (pornography, masturbation, sexual promiscuity, etc.) or are experiencing sexual difficulty and intimacy in your marriage, pray as follows:

Lord,
   I ask You to reveal to my mind every sexual use of my body as an instrument of unrighteousness. In Jesus' precious name, I pray. Amen.

As the Lord brings to your mind every sexual use of your body, whether it was done to you (rape, incest, or any sexual abuse) or willingly by you, renounce every occasion:

Lord,
I renounce (name the specific use of your body) with (name the person) and ask You to break that bond.

Now commit your body to the Lord by praying:

Lord,
I renounce all these uses of my body as an instrument of unrighteousness and by so doing ask You to break all bondages Satan has brought into my life through that involvement. I confess my participation. I now present my body to You as a living sacrifice, holy and acceptable unto You, and I reserve the sexual use of my body only for marriage. I renounce the lie of Satan that my body is not clean, that it is dirty or in any way unacceptable as a result of my past sexual experiences. Lord, I thank You that You have totally cleansed and forgiven me, that You love and accept me unconditionally. Therefore, I can accept myself. And I choose to do so, to accept myself and my body as cleansed. In Jesus' name. Amen.

Special Prayers for Specific Problems

Homosexuality

Lord,
I renounce the lie that You have created me or anyone else to be homosexual, and I affirm that You clearly forbid homosexual behavior. I accept myself as a child of God and declare that You created me a man (woman). I renounce any bondages of Satan that have perverted my relationships with others. I announce that I am free to relate to the opposite sex in the way that You intended. In Jesus' name. Amen.

Abortion

Lord,

I confess that I did not assume stewardship of the life You entrusted to me and I ask your forgiveness. I choose to accept your forgiveness, and I now commit that child to You for Your care in eternity. In Jesus' name. Amen.

Suicidal Tendencies

Lord,

I renounce suicidal thoughts and any attempts I have made to take my own life or in any way injure myself. I renounce the lie that life is hopeless and that I can find peace and freedom by taking my own life. Satan is a thief, and he comes to steal, kill, and destroy. I choose to be a good steward of the physical life that You have entrusted to me. In Jesus' name, I pray. Amen.

Eating Disorders or Cutting on Yourself

Lord,

I renounce the lie that my value as a person is dependent upon my physical beauty, my weight, or size. I renounce cutting myself, vomiting, using laxatives, or starving myself as a means of cleansing myself of evil or altering my appearance. I announce that only the blood of the Lord Jesus Christ cleanses me from sin. I accept the reality that there may be sin present in me due to the lies I have believed and the wrongful use of my body, but I renounce the lie that I am evil or that any part of my body is evil. My body is the temple of the Holy Spirit and I belong to You, Lord. I receive Your love and acceptance of me. In Jesus' name. Amen.

Substance Abuse

Lord,

I confess that I have misused substances (alcohol, tobacco, food, prescription or street drugs) for the purpose of pleasure, to escape reality, or to cope with difficult situations resulting in the abuse of my body, the harmful programming of my mind, and the quenching of the Holy Spirit. I ask Your forgiveness. I renounce any satanic connection or influence in my life through my misuse of chemicals or food. I cast my anxiety onto Christ Who loves me, and I commit myself to no longer yield to substance abuse but to the Holy Spirit. I ask You, Heavenly Father, to fill me with Your Holy Spirit. In Jesus' name. Amen.

Drivenness and Perfectionism

Lord,

I renounce the lie that my self-worth is dependent upon my ability to perform. I announce the truth that my identity and sense of worth is found in who I am as Your child. I renounce seeking the approval and acceptance of other people, and I choose to believe that I am already approved and accepted in Christ because of His death and resurrection for me. I choose to believe the truth that I have been saved, not by deeds done in righteousness, but according to Your mercy. I choose to believe that I am no longer under the curse of the law because Christ became a curse for me. I receive the free gift of life in Christ and choose to abide in Him. I renounce striving for perfection by living under the law. By Your grace, Heavenly Father, I choose from this day forward to walk by faith according to what You have said is true by the power of Your Holy Spirit.

Plaguing Fears

Dear Heavenly Father,

I acknowledge You as the only legitimate fear object in my life. You are the only omnipresent (always present) and omniscient (all-knowing) God and the only means by which all other fears can be expelled. You are my sanctuary. You have not given me a spirit of timidity, but of power and love and discipline. I confess that I have allowed the fear of man and the fear of death to exercise control over my life instead of trusting in You. I now renounce all other fear objects and worship You only. I pray that You would fill me with Your Holy Spirit that I may live my life and speak your Word with boldness. In Jesus' name, I pray. Amen.

After you have confessed all known sin, pray:

Dear Heavenly Father,

I now confess these sins to You and claim through the blood of the Lord Jesus Christ my forgiveness and cleansing. I cancel all ground that evil spirits have gained through my willful involvement in sin. I ask this in the wonderful name of my Lord and Savior, Jesus Christ. Amen.

STEP 7:
Acquiescence vs. Renunciation

Acquiescence is passively giving in or agreeing without consent. The last step to freedom is to renounce the sins of your ancestors and any curses which may have been placed on you. In giving the Ten Commandments, God said: "You shall not make for yourself an idol, or any likeness of what is in heaven above or on the earth beneath or in the water under the earth. You shall not worship them or serve them; for I, the Lord your God, am a jealous God, visiting the iniquity of the fathers on the children, on the third and fourth generations of those who hate Me" (Ex. 20:4-5).

Familiar spirits can be passed on from one generation to the next if not renounced and if your new spiritual heritage in Christ is not proclaimed. You are not guilty for the sin of any ancestor, but because of their sin, Satan may have gained access to your family. This is not to deny that many problems are transmitted genetically or acquired from an immoral atmosphere. All three conditions can predispose an individual to a particular sin. In addition, deceived people may try to curse you, or satanic groups may try to target you. You have all the authority and protection you need in Christ to stand against such curses and assignments. Ask the Lord to reveal to your mind the sins and iniquities of your ancestors by praying the following prayer:

> Dear Heavenly Father,
> I thank You that I am a new creation in Christ. I desire to obey Your command to honor my mother and my father, but I also acknowledge that my physical heritage has not been perfect. I ask you to reveal to my mind the sins and iniquities of my ancestors in order to confess, renounce, and forsake them. In Jesus' name, I pray. Amen.

Now claim your position and protection in Christ by making the following declaration verbally, and then by humbling yourself before God in prayer.

Declaration

I here and now reject and disown all the sins and iniquities of my ancestors, including (<u>name them</u>). As one who has been delivered from the power of darkness and translated into the kingdom of God's dear Son, I cancel out all demonic working that has been passed on to me from my ancestors. As one who has been crucified and raised with Jesus Christ and who sits with Him in heavenly places, I renounce all satanic assignments that are directed toward me and my ministry, and I cancel every curse that Satan and his workers have put on me. I announce to Satan and all his forces that Christ became a curse for me (Gal. 3:13) when He died for my sins on the cross. I reject any and every way in which Satan may claim ownership of me. I belong to the Lord Jesus Christ who purchased me with His own blood. I reject all other blood sacrifices whereby Satan may claim ownership of me. I declare myself to be eternally and completely signed over and committed to the Lord Jesus Christ. By the authority I have in Jesus Christ, I now command every familiar spirit and every enemy of the Lord Jesus Christ that is in or around me to leave my presence. I commit myself to my Heavenly Father to do His will from this day forward.

Prayer

Dear Heavenly Father,

I come to You as Your child purchased by the blood of the Lord Jesus Christ. You are the Lord of the universe and the Lord of my life. I submit my body to You as an instrument of righteousness, a living sacrifice, that I may glorify You in my body. I now ask You to fill me with Your Holy Spirit. I commit myself to the renewing of my mind in order to prove that Your will is good, perfect, and acceptable for me. All this I do in the name and authority of the Lord Jesus Christ. Amen.

Once you have secured your freedom by going through these seven steps, you may find demonic influences attempting reentry days or even months later. One person shared that she heard a spirit say to her mind "I'm back" two days after she had been set free. "No, you're not!" she proclaimed aloud. The attack ceased immediately. One victory does not constitute winning the war. Freedom must be maintained. After completing these steps, one jubilant lady asked, "Will I always be like this?" I told her that she would stay free as long as she remained in right relationship with God. "Even if you slip and fall," I encouraged, "you know how to get right with God again."

One victim of incredible atrocities shared this illustration: "It's like being forced to play a game with an ugly stranger in my own home. I kept losing and wanted to quit, but the ugly stranger wouldn't let me. Finally I called the police (a higher authority), and they came and escorted the stranger out. He knocked on the door trying to regain entry, but this time **I recognized his voice** and didn't let him in." What a beautiful illustration of gaining freedom in Christ. We call upon Jesus, the ultimate authority, and He escorts the enemy out of our lives. Know the truth, stand firm, and resist the evil one. Seek out good Christian fellowship, and commit yourself to regular times of Bible study and prayer. God loves you and will never leave or forsake you.

After Care

Freedom must be maintained. You have won a very important battle in an ongoing war. Freedom is yours as long as you keep choosing truth and standing firm in the strength of the Lord. If new memories should surface or if you become aware of "lies" that you have believed or other non-Christian experiences you have had, renounce them and choose the truth. Some have found it helpful to go through the steps again. As you do, read the instructions carefully.

For your encouragement and further study, read *Victory Over the Darkness* (adult or youth version), *The Bondage Breaker* (adult or youth version), and *Released from Bondage*. If you are a parent, read *The Seduction of Our Children*. *Walking in the Light* (formerly *Walking Through the Darkness*) was written to help people understand God's guidance and discern counterfeit guidance. Also, to maintain your freedom, we suggest the following:

• Seek legitimate Christian fellowship where you can walk in the light and speak the truth in love.

• Study your Bible daily. Memorize key verses.

- Take every thought captive to the obedience of Christ. Assume responsibility for your thought life, reject the lie, choose the truth, and stand firm in your position in Christ.

- Don't drift away! It is very easy to get lazy in your thoughts and revert back to old habit patterns of thinking. Share your struggles openly with a trusted friend. You need at least one friend who will stand with you.

- Don't expect another person to fight your battle for you. Others can help but they can't think, pray, read the Bible, or choose the truth for you.

- Continue to seek your identity and sense of worth in Christ. Read *Living Free in Christ* and the devotional, *Daily in Christ*. Renew your mind with the truth that your acceptance, security, and significance is in Christ by saturating your mind with the following truths. Read the entire list of who you are "in Christ" and the Doctrinal Affirmation (in Step 2) aloud morning and evening over the next several weeks (and look up the verses referenced).

- Commit yourself to daily prayer. You can pray these suggested prayers often and with confidence:

Daily Prayer

Dear Heavenly Father,
I honor You as my sovereign Lord. I acknowledge that You are always present with me. You are the only all-powerful and only-wise God. You are kind and loving in all Your ways. I love You and thank You that I am united with Christ and spiritually alive in Him. I choose not to love the world, and I crucify the flesh and all its passions.

I thank You for the life that I now have in Christ, and I ask You to fill me with Your Holy Spirit that I may live my life free from sin. I declare my dependence upon

You, and I take my stand against Satan and all his lying ways. I choose to believe the truth, and I refuse to be discouraged. You are the God of all hope, and I am confident that You will meet my needs as I seek to live according to Your Word. I express with confidence that I can live a responsible life through Christ who strengthens me.

I now take my stand against Satan and command him and all his evil spirits to depart from me. I put on the whole armor of God. I submit my body as a living sacrifice and renew my mind by the living Word of God in order that I may prove that the will of God is good, acceptable, and perfect. I ask these things in the precious name of my Lord and Savior, Jesus Christ. Amen.

Bedtime Prayer

Thank You, Lord,

You have brought me into Your family and have blessed me with every spiritual blessing in the heavenly realms in Christ. Thank You for providing this time of renewal through sleep. I accept it as part of Your perfect plan for Your children, and I trust You to guard my mind and my body during my sleep. As I have meditated on You and Your truth during this day, I choose to let these thoughts continue in my mind while I am asleep. I commit myself to You for Your protection from every attempt of Satan or his emissaries to attack me during sleep. I commit myself to You as my Rock, my Fortress, and my Resting Place. I pray in the strong name of the Lord Jesus Christ. Amen.

Cleansing Home/Apartment

After removing all articles of false worship from home/apartment, pray aloud in every room if necessary.

Heavenly Father,

We acknowledge that You are Lord of heaven and earth. In Your sovereign power and love, You have given us all things richly to enjoy. Thank You for this place to live. We claim this home for our family as a place of spiritual safety and protection from all the attacks of the enemy. As children of God seated with Christ in the heavenly realm, we command every evil spirit claiming ground in the structures and furnishings of this place, based on the activities of previous occupants, to leave and never return. We renounce all curses and spells utilized against this place. We ask You, Heavenly Father, to post guardian angels around this home (apartment, condo, room, etc.) to guard it from attempts of the enemy to enter and disturb Your purposes for us. We thank You, Lord, for doing this, and pray in the name of the Lord Jesus Christ. Amen.

Living in a Non-Christian Environment

After removing all articles of false worship from your room, pray aloud in the space allotted to you.

Thank You, Heavenly Father,

For my place to live and be renewed by sleep. I ask You to set aside my room (portion of my room) as a place of spiritual safety for me. I renounce any allegiance given to false gods or spirits by other occupants, and I renounce any claim to this room (space) by Satan based on activities of past occupants or me. On the basis of my position as a child of God and a joint-heir with Christ who has all authority in heaven and on earth, I command all evil spirits to leave this place and never to return. I ask You, Heavenly Father, to appoint guardian angels to protect me while I live here. I pray this in the name of the Lord Jesus Christ. Amen.

IN CHRIST

I AM ACCEPTED

John 1:12	I am God's child.
John 15:15	I am Christ's friend.
Rom. 5:1	I have been justified.
1 Cor. 6:17	I am united with the Lord, and I am one spirit with Him.
1 Cor. 6:19-20	I have been bought with a price. I belong to God.
1 Cor. 12:27	I am a member of Christ's body.
Eph. 1:1	I am a saint.
Eph. 1:5	I have been adopted as God's child.
Eph. 2:18	I have direct access to God through the Holy Spirit.
Col. 1:14	I have been redeemed and forgiven of all my sins.
Col. 2:10	I am complete in Christ.

I AM SECURE

Rom. 8:1-2	I am free forever from condemnation.
Rom. 8:28	I am assured that all things work together for good.
Rom. 8:31-34	I am free from any condemning charges against me.
Rom. 8:35-39	I cannot be separated from the love of God.
2 Cor. 1:21-22	I have been established, anointed, and sealed by God.
Col. 3:3	I am hidden with Christ in God.
Phil. 1:6	I am confident that the good work that God has begun in me will be perfected.
Phil. 3:20	I am a citizen of heaven.
2 Tim. 1:7	I have not been given a spirit of fear but of power, love, and a sound mind.

| Heb. 4:16 | I can find grace and mercy to help in time of need. |
| 1 Jn. 5:18 | I am born of God and the evil one cannot touch me. |

I AM SIGNIFICANT

Matt. 5:13-14	I am the salt and light of the earth.
John 15:1, 5	I am a branch of the true vine, a channel of His life.
John 15:16	I have been chosen and appointed to bear fruit.
Acts 1:8	I am a personal witness of Christ's.
1 Cor. 3:16	I am God's temple.
2 Cor. 5:17-21	I am a minister of reconciliation for God.
2 Cor. 6:1	I am God's co-worker (1 Cor. 3:9).
Eph. 2:6	I am seated with Christ in the heavenly realm.
Eph. 2:10	I am God's workmanship.
Eph. 3:12	I may approach God with freedom and confidence.
Phil. 4:13	I can do all things through Christ who strengthens me.

Many additional resources are available from:

Freedom in Christ Ministries
9051 Executive Park Dr. Ste. 503
Knoxville, TN 37923
Ph: 865-342-4000 - Fax: 865-342-4001
Email: info@ficm.org
Web: www.ficm.org